Blue is collecting letter sounds in her sound machine. She's looking for words that begin with every letter of the alphabet. Can you help her? You'll need the special decoder included in this book. Use it to see the answers hidden next to Blue's pawprints.

Blue is looking for the Bb sound. She found some bunnies. Bunny begins with the Bb sound.

Practice saying **Bb** then help Blue add it to the sound machine by tracing **Bb** on the sound disk.

Do you see anything else that begins with the Bb sound? Circle the pictures and use your decoder to check your answers.

A buzzing bee begins with **Bb**. What other letters sounds can you find here? Say the name of each picture and circle the letter sound that it begins with.

Ll Mm

Uu Ii

4

Rr Dd

Aa Oo

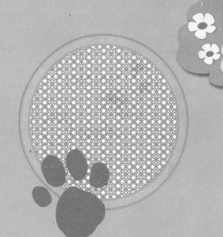

Blue knows that every letter has two forms – capital and lowercase. And both forms of a letter have the same sound. Will you help Blue match the letters with the same sound? Draw a line from each capital letter to the matching lowercase letter.

Blue is looking for something that starts with the Ww sound. Look, she found a wagon! Will you write Ww on Blue's sound disk? Wonderful!

Practice saying the Ww sound.

What other letter sounds can you help Blue find at the playground? Say the name of each picture and circle the letter sound that it begins with. Use your decoder to check your answers.

Ss Mm

Gg Jj

Pp Nn

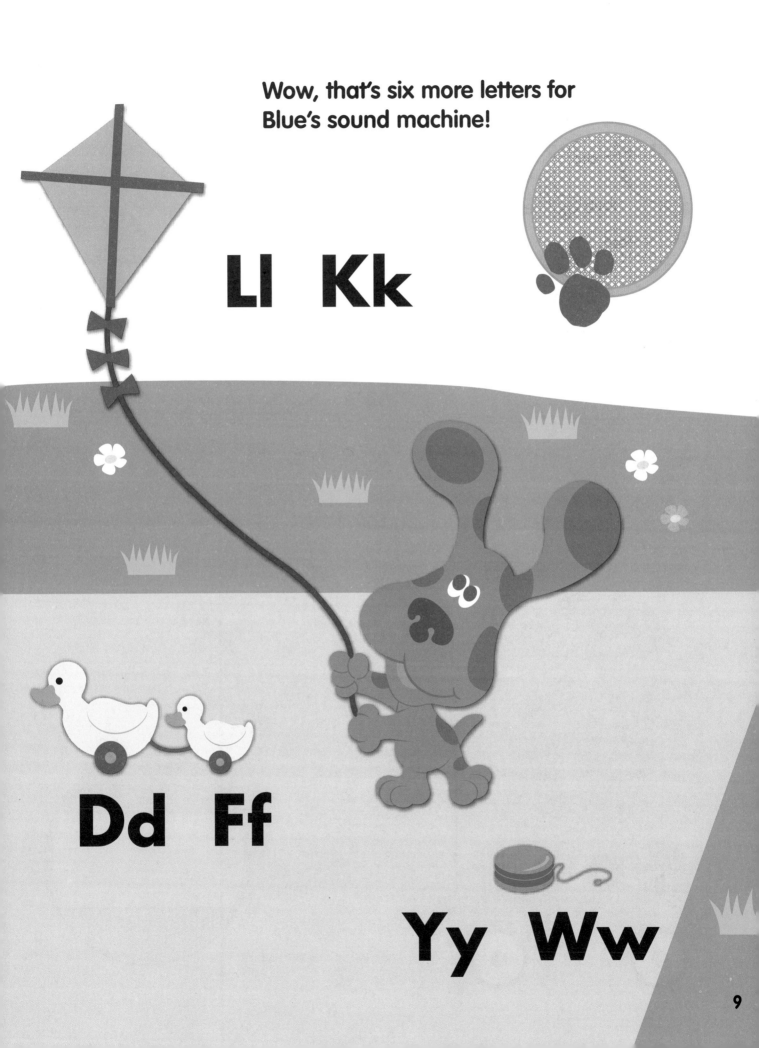

Wow, that's six more letters for Blue's sound machine!

Ll Kk

Dd Ff

Yy Ww

9

Hey, Blue found something that starts with the Hh sound. Helmet! Blue always wears a helmet when she rides her scooter. Look, Periwinkle has a helmet on, too!

Practice saying the Hh sound and write Hh on the sound disk.

Blue found some more capital and lowercase letters to match. Will you help her? Color the block with the capital letter that is the same as the lowercase letter in each row. Remember, matching capital and lowercase letters have the same sound.

d	B	D	R
n	N	W	M
h	R	J	H
k	W	K	A
j	L	S	J

11

Blue is looking for things that begin with the Gg and Vv sounds. She found a garden – full of vegetables! Write Vv and Gg on different sound disks. Very good!

Help Blue find more letter sounds in the vegetable garden. Circle the vegetables that start with the Tt, Cc, and Ll sounds. Color the friend whose name starts with the Pp sound. Look next to Blue's pawprints to see if you're right.

Uh oh, it's starting to rain. Blue found the perfect Uu sound that goes with rain. Umbrella!

Practice saying the Uu sound and write Uu on one of Blue's sound disks.

Blue found some pictures of things that begin with the same sounds as her friends' names. Will you help her match them? Draw a line from Blue's friends to the pictures that start with the same sound.

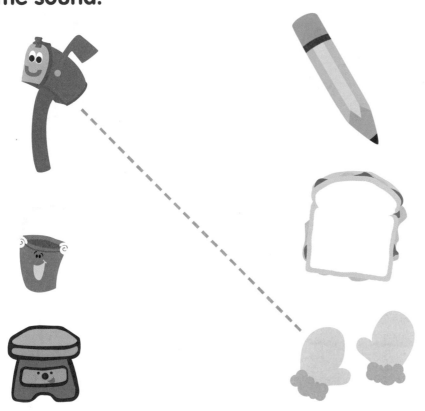

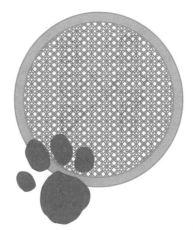

Blue made a rainy day picture that looks just like the weather outside. She drew a zigzag bolt of lightning for the Zz sound at the beginning of zigzag. Find and color the zigzag lightning bolt.

Do you see a picture that begins with the Qq sound?
Quick! Circle it.

Practice saying the Qq and Zz letter sounds.

Maybe you can help Blue find some more letter sounds in the kitchen. Use the letters on the refrigerator to fill in the beginning sound of each word. Circle the letters that you use.

_____ ggs

_____ ork

f x o r e r a y

_____lives

Blue used the letters that were left on the refrigerator to make a word that begins with the Xx sound. It's x-ray! Write Xx on the sound disk. Excellent!

Practice saying the Xx sound.

Blue found some things in the kitchen that have the same letter sound. Will you help her sort them? Color the pictures that start with the same sound in each row.

carrot	donut	corn
pie	pumpkin	apple
cup	bowl	banana

Blue's letter sound collection is all done. Now she wants to play it on her sound machine. Help her write the letters for all the sounds she found. Say the name of each picture and write the letter sound that it begins with.

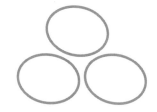   

 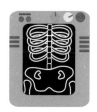  

Zz

Great job! You helped Blue find words that begin with every letter of the alphabet.